The Secret Benefits of
Onion and Garlic

The Secret Benefits of
Onion and Garlic

VIJAYA KUMAR

NEW DAWN PRESS, INC.
USA• UK• INDIA

NEW DAWN PRESS GROUP
Published by New Dawn Press Group
New Dawn Press, Inc., 244 South Randall Rd # 90, Elgin, IL 60123
e-mail: sales@newdawnpress.com

New Dawn Press, 2 Tintern Close, Slough, Berkshire, SL1-2TB, UK
e-mail: salesuk@newdawnpress.org

New Dawn Press (An Imprint of Sterling Publishers (P) Ltd)
A-59, Okhla Industrial Area, Phase-II, New Delhi-110020, India
e-mail: info@sterlingpublishers.com
www.sterlingpublishers.com

The Secret Benefits of Onion and Garlic
© 2006, Sterling Publishers (P) Ltd
ISBN 978-1-84557-533-5
Reprint 2007

PRINTED IN INDIA

Contents

Contents

Introduction

An onion can make people cry, but there's no vegetable that can make them laugh!

—*Anonymous*

The onion family can bring tears to your eyes, literally. Despite the tears, onions and garlic are popular vegetables or condiments, and favoured by the home grower and cooks. Indeed, what would a kitchen be without the distinctively pungent smell and taste of onions and garlic filling out the flavours of almost every type of cuisine imaginable!

The word 'onion' comes from the Latin word *unio* meaning 'single' or 'one', because the onion plant produces a single bulb, unlike its cousin, the garlic, that produces many small bulbs. The name also describes the many separate, concentrically arranged layers of the onion.

Garlic is a native Germanic word, being composed of two elements: *gar* meaning 'spear', referring to the pointed leaves, and *lie,* meaning either leek or onion. Being efficient preservatives, leek and its relatives were considered powerful magic plants by Germans.

In classical Latin, garlic was termed *allium,* which is still the botanical genus name for garlic, onion, leek, shallot, chives, etc. Derived from a Celtic root, they all mean 'burning, pungent'.

Onions and their relatives are botanically known as *alliums,* a plant genus that has been classified at different times as belonging to the lily family, the *amaryllis* family, or *Alliaceae* family. There are more than 500 alliums. All of the edible species are bubbling plants with a characteristic pungent smell or taste, which is produced once their layers of skin are cut.

Garlic (*Allium Sativum*) has lovingly been dubbed 'The Stinking Rose'. If you go back to the Anglo-Saxon roots of the word 'garlic', you come up with 'gar-leac'. *Leac* was the term for any plant of the allium genus. Onions were 'ynne-leac', and leeks 'pot-leac'. *Gar* meant 'spear' and referred to the spearhead shape of the cloves. 'Clove' comes from the Old English *chifu,* from which the modern word 'cleave' derives. When you cleave the garlic head you get cloves.

Onion and garlic are a borderline case between spices and vegetables. They are indispensable ingredients to nearly every cuisine of the world, and used for large spectrum of different dishes. Today, they rank sixth among the world's leading vegetable crops. In the United States, Gilroy (California) promotes itself as the 'Garlic Capital of the World'.

Onion and garlic have been in use by man for centuries. He has found quite a number of uses of them for many of his ailments. Ayurveda, Unani and folklore medicines offer a host of diverse uses and efficiencies. Modern day investigations corroborate their benefits and uses in medicine. Classical authors like Charaka, Sushruta, Harita, etc., extensively mention the use of onion, in their works. The Chinese, the Egyptians, the Hebrew, the Greeks and the Romans have all used garlic as an item of diet or medicine. Hippocrates, the Father of Modern Medicine, was convinced that it cured all sorts of digestive disorders, while Homer, the great Greek epic poet, raved about its divine properties. Aristophanes, a famous Greek dramatist, mentioned in a passage that garlic offered great strength to the Greek soldiers during was. Pliny, the Roman historian, extolled the use of garlic.

In bygone days, onions and garlic were believed to have the best curative powers. Today, they are recognised all over the world as all-round wonder drugs for the treatment of several diseases. In fact, during the American Civil War, General Ulysses S. Grant sent a telegram to the War Department, "I will not move my army without onions!" The next day he got them!

Onions and garlic are known to serve as anticoagulants, anti-depressants, pain-killers, mucus removers, insulin stimulators, antibiotics, and anti-inflammators.

1
Origin and History

Onion

It is difficult to say when exactly the onion came into being, but it is believed to have originated in ancient Egypt, Greece, Rome, India and China. Due to its wide cultivation all over the world, its origins are uncertain. It has been traced to both south-west Siberia and Sicily, while a few believe it to have originated in Central Asia, possibly in the Iran-Pakistan region.

Though most historians believe it could have originated in the Asia-Europe landmass, it is likely that it may have been growing wild on every continent. Dating back to 3500 BC, onions were one of the few foods that did not spoil during the winter months. Our ancestors must have recognised the vegetable's durability, and begun growing onions for food.

In Egypt

Onions are cooking ingredients around the world, and have been used for thousands of years. Huge quantities of them were consumed by ancient Egyptians, and several tombs of pharaohs included carvings of onion and garlic, intended for meals in the After Life.

Today, strong-tasting onions are an essential part of the typical Egyptian diet, which has basically no other pungent species.

The onion became more than just food after arriving in Egypt. The ancient Egyptians worshipped the onion, believing that its spherical shape and concentric rings symbolised eternity.

Of all the vegetables that had the images created from precious metals by Egyptian artists, only the onion was made out of gold.

The onion is depicted on tombs that were built as early as 3200 BC. It has been found in mummies, and were used in religious and funerary offerings.

The Egyptians also used them as currency to pay workers who built the pyramids. They placed the onions in tombs of kings, such as Tutankhanem, so that they could carry these gifts, bestowed with spiritual significance, with them to the After Life.

Of all the foods in the plants kingdom, onions set the record for the most frequent appearance in ancient Egyptian art. It certainly is no wonder since they were the staple food of the poor, along with bread and beer. Onions often appear in Egyptian art as a sacrifice that appeared on their altars.

Strange as it seems today, in ancient Egypt, a basket of onions was considered a very respectable funeral offering, rating only second to the highly revered basket of bread.

One cannot deny the senses. The rich found the odour downright disgusting. In spite of their negative attitudes, though, this odorous vegetable was activated in the gardens of the ancient kings from 2100 BC to 716 BC from Ur to Babylon.

From ancient history up to the nineteenth century, onions were relegated as the food for the poor. The code of Hammurabi, known as the ancient law of Mesopotamia, shows great concern for the needy by providing them a monthly ration of bread and onions, a ration that comprised the mainstay of the peasant diet. As disagreeable as the onion was to the aristocrats, the peasants devoured them completely raw.

In Europe

In Europe, onions are known since the Bronze Age. Together with garlic, onion is mentioned in the oldest part of the Bible, the Pentateuch. The status of the onion rose after the French Onion Soup was made popular by Stanislaus I, a former king of Poland.

By the seventeenth century, Europeans were enjoying onions as salad ingredient and a breakfast health food.

While they were popular with the ancient Greeks and Romans, they were often dressed with extra seasonings, since many people did not find them spicy enough. Yet, it was their pungency that made them popular among poor people throughout the world, who could freely use this inexpensive vegetable to spice up their meals.

Onions also played a role during the period Alexander the Great was leading his armies in conquest of other lands. It was believed that, if one ate strong food, one would become strong. Alexander fed his men onions, believing they would increase their strength and courage.

In ancient Greece and Rome, the common folk relished their onions, and even ate them raw. Apicius, Imperial Rome's first cookbook author, never featured onions in his cuisine of the wealthy, but only used them as flavourings in sauces, or to enhance a mixed dish or a dressing.

The common folk frequently started their day with a heavy serving of raw onions on bread, a recurring theme throughout the peasant world, and one abhorred by the upper classes. In fact, they were so appreciated that Emperor Charlimagne ordered onions to be planted in his royal gardens. They were written into the French feudal deeds, and strings of onions were even accepted as payment for the use of land.

In America

It is believed that Christopher Columbus brought onions to the West Indies, and from there, their cultivation spread in the Americas.

Had it not been for onions, the civil war in the United States may have turned out differently. General

S. Grant, who headed the Union forces, sent a note to the War Department that read, "I will not move my troops without onions." He promptly received three cartloads. He also employed the juice of onions medicinally as a wound healer.

American cowboys flavoured another native onion, the prairie onion, that they called 'skunk egg'. No doubt, it earned this descriptive name because of its powerful odour. Apart from odour the onion lends exceptional flavour to any raw or cooked dish, and was always included in a favourite cowboy plat du jour, called son-of-a-bitch stew!

The varieties of onions have all strong smells and pungent flavours. So it is no surprise that native tribes learned to use these as foods or as seasonings. Examples of uses by native peoples are recorded from North America in their north-western regions, where numerous Indian tribes collected and consumed several species of native onions. Cooked onions were eaten immediately, used as an ingredient to flavour meat and salmon meals, or dried in strings for use at a later time.

In California, wild onions were rubbed on as an insect repellent.

In India

Onions have been revered throughout time, not only for their culinary use, but also for their therapeutic properties.

As early as the sixth century, onions were used as a medicine in India. The *Garuda Purana* mentions onion as *palandu,* the Sanskrit word for onion. Its use has been variously described by the great Indian sages, Maharishi Atreya and Lord Dhanavantari.

It also features in the Quran, and many other literary treatises.

Cultivation

For nearly 4,000 years, it is known to be under cultivation. In fact, it is now known only as a cultivated crop, there being no wild varieties. It is propagated either by planting the bulbs, or sowing the seeds.

Onion is now cultivated in most parts of the world, including India, Malaysia, Spain, the Philippines, Indonesia, Myanmar, China, Egypt, Russia, West and East Africa, South and Central America, the United States of America, and the Caribbeans.

In India, this crop is mainly cultivated in Maharashtra, Gujarat, Tamil Nadu, Andhra Pradesh, Bihar and Punjab.

Garlic

Although garlic may not always bring good luck, protect against evil, or ward off vampires, as believed in the olden days, it is guaranteed to transform any meal into a bold, aromatic and healthy culinary experience.

Everyone can think badly about garlic and onions—the garlic breath or onion breath so hated on a date, or tears brought on when raw onions are sliced. Used for centuries around the world for everything, from numbing toothaches to warding off vampires, a whole new generation is taking to garlic with a passion.

Garlic is native to Central Asia, but its use spread across the world more than 5,000 years ago, before recorded history. From the earliest times it has been used as an article of diet.

In Egypt

Garlic formed part of the food of the Israelites in Egypt, and of the labourers employed by Emperor Cheops in the construction of his pyramid.

According to the Roman writer Pliny, garlics were invoked, by the Egyptians as deities at the time of taking oaths. Since the inhabitants of Pelusium in lower Egypt worshipped both garlic and onion, they held these two vegetables in aversion as food.

The Egyptians placed clay models of garlic bulbs in the tomb of Tutankhamen.

The Great Giza pyramid builders were fed their daily share of garlic to give them strength, vitality and nourishment, in 2600 BC.

The Bible mentions garlic as a food the Hebrews enjoyed during their sojourn in Egypt.

Ancient Egyptians seem to have been the first to cultivate the garlic plant that played an important role in their culture.

It is still grown in Egypt, where, however, the Syrian variety is the most esteemed.

In Europe

Garlic has been a common spice in Europe since the days of the Roman Empire. It was largely consumed by the ancient Greek and Roman soldiers, sailors and rural classes.

Garlic was rare in traditional English cookery, and a much more common ingredient in southern Europe.

It was fed to the athletes before sporting events, as it was believed to enhance their endurance and strength.

The ancient Greeks placed the garlic on the piles of stones at crossroads as, a supper of Hecate, the goddess of the underworld, and companion of Persephone.

In 1916, the British government asked for tons of garlic bulbs, offering one shilling a pound for as much as could be produced. A great quantity of it was used for the control of suppuration in wounds. The raw juice was extracted, diluted with water, and put on swabs of sterilised sphagnum moss which was applied to the wounds. Where this treatment was given, it has been proved that there has never been one single case of sepsis of septic results. Consequently, the lives of tens of thousands were saved by this one miraculous herb. That was many years ago, and this practice is still prevalent in many rural and backward areas in the world.

Garlic was the principal ingredient in the famous Four Thieves Vinegar which was adapted so successfully at Marseilles for protection against the plague when it prevailed there in 1772. It is said that this originated, with four thieves who confessed that, while protected, by the liberal use of aromatic garlic vinegar during the plague, they plundered the dead bodies of the victims with complete safety!

It is stated that during an outbreak of an infectious fever in certain poor quarters of London early in the last century, the French priests, who constantly used garlic in all their dishes visited the very worst cases with impunity, while the English clergy caught the infection, and in many instances, fell victims to the disease.

Few plants have more legends than garlic. A Muhammaden legend related that "when satan stepped out from the Garden of Eden after the fall of man, garlic sprang up from the spot where he placed his left foot, and onion from that where his right touched."

In Europe, it was believed to be protection against the 'evil eye', and to make witches and vampires disappear at its very sight.

Racers who chewed a bit of garlic thought they could not be beaten.

Hungarian jockeys attached a piece of garlic to their horse's bits to prevent the competitors from winning.

In Bram stoker's *Dracula,* a doctor strewed the room with garlic, and hung a necklace of garlic around a woman's throat in the belief that garlic would repel vampires.

During the Dark Ages, people believed it could ward off the plague, and wore garlands of it as protection.

Virgil, the Roman poet (70 BC), in his Eclogues, states that garlic was part of the entertainment served by Nestor to his guest, Machaon. He also tells us that it was owing to the virtues of garlic that Ulysses owed his escape from being changed by Circe into a pig, like each of his companions.

Galen speaks very highly of garlic, eulogising it as the 'theriac' or 'heal all'.

Chaucer calls it 'theriac' as do several old English botanists and herbalists.

Pliny gives an exceedingly long list of complaints in which it was considered beneficial.

Alexander Neckam, a writer of the twelfth century, recommends it as a palliative of the heat of the sun in field labour.

In Asia
Garlic was extensively used from India to East Asia, even before the Europeans arrived there.

By the sixth century BC, it was known to both India and China, the former using it for therapeutic purposes.

In America
Garlic came to the West with some of the first European explorers, and its use spread rapidly.

In the United States, it was first cultivated in New Orleans by French settlers.

Missionaries brought it to California, where it is grown extensively today, as the state's wild climate is suitable for its growth.

Recent demand for high-quality garlic has prompted an interest in growing it for niche markets in the upper Midwest.

It is strange though that garlic does not figure as an official remedy in the United States' Pharmacopeia.

Cultivation

Currently, China, South Korea, India, Spain and the United States are among the top commercial producers of garlic. Other countries which grow it extensively for domestic use are the Philippines, Ethiopia, Kenya, Brazil and Mexico.

In India it has long been cultivated in all parts of the country as an important crop.

2

Description and Propagation

Onions

Onions may bring tears to your eyes, and a pungency to your breath, but they will certainly delight your taste buds!

Onions lovers throughout the world are weeping, and they simply can't help it! What is this phenomenon all about, you wonder? It boils down to a few biting facts, recognising that onions, a mere vegetable, have that certain power to bring us to tears.

Historically, the onion is nothing to cry about! Over many centuries, it occupied an exalted position as a work of art as well as a food. Not many people today would burst into tears if they were asked to

The garlic plant is shorter than the onion plant, growing to just about a foot in height.

The leaves in a clump are much smaller than those of the onion, but otherwise, are like them, being long, narrow, slender, and rather flattish. They are half an inch in width, and taper upwards elongatedly.

The scape, being green, quite long and hollow, bears an umbrella-like cluster at its end. This has numerous flowers that bloom in the cold season.

In the underground, at the base of the plant, are the bulbs, formed by the basal regions of the leaves. These bulbs are called garlic.

Each bulb has about eight to ten cloves which are also enclosed in a thin, white, papery, non-succulent and inedible skin. From these, new bulbs can be procured, by planting them out in late water or early summer.

Although garlic cloves have a firm texture, they can be easily cut or crushed.

The taste of the garlic is like no other crop—it hits the palate with a hot pungency that is shadowed by a very subtle background sweetness.

While an elephant garlic has larger cloves, it is more closely related to the leek, and therefore does not offer the full benefits of the regular garlic.

Garlic cloves are off-white in colour, while the enclosing paper-like sheath can be white, off-white or pinkish.

The tear-drop-shaped garlic bulbs range in size. However, they usually average around two inches in height, and two in width at their widest point.

The cultivated garlic plant does not produce seeds, but is grown from bulbs. These bulbs are the part of the plant most commonly eaten, though some cooks also use the early spring shoots. The roots of the plant are adventitious, and rather irregular.

Garlic, like the onion, grows under much the same conditions, with a well-drained, moderately clayey loam, and a high elevation. It requires a cool, moist period during growth.

The obscurely keeled leaves, a deciduous spathe, and a globose umbel of whitish flowers, among which are small bulbils, lend the plant an attractive appearance.

Storage Onions

The storage onions have firm flesh, dry and crackly outer skins, and pungent flavours.

These onions are well dried or 'cured' for a brief period before being stored for several months.

Spanish Onions are a variety of very large storage type, distinguished by their mild flavour and skin colour, which ranges from yellow to purple.

There are no nutritional differences among these types.

Onions are available in red, white or yellow varieties, wild or pungent, deep globe or flat globe, and as seed, sets or transplants. There are more yellow onion varieties to chose from than reds or whites.

Yellow Onions

Yellow onions make up more than 75 per cent of the world's production of onions.

The Maui Onions are golden yellow, sweet and juicy, grown on the Island of Maui, Hawaii. They are very sweet, have a high water content, and usually are heavy in weight.

These onions are usually shaped like a flattened globe. They are excellent for onion rings.

They are full-flavoured, and are a reliable standby for cooking almost anything.

They turn into a rich, dark brown colour when cooked, and give French Onion Soup its tangy, sweet flavour.

Red Onions

The red onion, with its wonderful colour, is a good choice for fresh uses in grilling or broiling.

White Onions

White onions are the traditional ones used in classic Mexican cuisine.

These onions have a pale golden colour, and have a sweet flavour when sautéed.

White onions are more preferred for medicinal properties.

Pearl Onions

Also called white onions, the pearl onions are actually white pearl-shaped bulbs from different varieties.

The plants are so densely planted that they attain a size of only one inch or less in width.

The bulbs too are used in seasoning food.

Leeks

Leeks have flat rather than tubular leaves, which are thick, broad and massive.

Only the white base of the plant is eaten, so it is customary to blanch the base by pulling the soil up around the stem to promote a longer white base.

Leeks may be eaten fresh, or used in cooked dishes. Their use in the kitchen is quite like that of the lettuce. Their leaf bases are mild flavoured.

Shallots

These too are perennial herbs that have clustered bulbs, and hollow, cylindrical leaves that are short and oval-shaped. The bulbs have a milder flavour than onions.

Some of the leaves may be cut at the ground level, and used as green onions.

Those plants, which are not heavily cut, will form many bulbs attached together in a clamp.

Scallions

Immature bulbing onions are called scallions. These have thick necks, and do not store well.

Welsh Onion

The Welsh Onion, also known as the Japanese Bunching Onion, is a white stemmed stone leek that is a native of Far East Asia.

It is a hardy perennial which does not form a real bulb, but only a small enlargement at the base.

It is used in salads, and for flavouring soups and stews.

Pickling Onions

In the United States, onion pickles are greatly favoured, and hence onions are grown for commercial purposes also.

In India, recently, a variety of small pink-cloured onion has been introduced for pickling.

Grown in Kolar and Bangalore of Karnataka State, and also in Cuddapah of Andhra Pradesh, these onions are characterised by their pungency and small bulbs.

Comparison of Onions

The characteristic smell of the bulb is present in all onions, but it is less in the white and big variety.

The white onions are milder in pungency, compared to the red ones.

rainfall, temperature, altitude, length and severity of winter, etc.

The hard-neck garlics were the original garlics, and the soft-necked ones were developed or cultivated over the centuries by growers, from the original hard-necks through a process of selection.

Hard-neck Garlic

Hard-neck garlics are considered to be the primitive, wild form.

They are generally easy to peel, and offer a wider span of tastes.

They produce a central stalk that is removed soon after it appears, so that heads reach full size.

The hard-neck garlic produces a woody, flower stalk.

The cloves, being much larger than the soft-neck ones, are easier to peel.

Garlics of this type have a more complex and interesting flavour than other varieties. This variety does not keep long.

1. Asiatic Garlic

The Asian Tempest is of the best-flavoured and hottest varieties.

The Bogatyr stays longer than most varieties of any type.

The Pitarelli is a variety that stays usable longer than most soft-necks.

The Siberian is flavourful, and good in cold climates.

In Bellary district of Karnataka in India, the Fowari and Rajalle Gaddi garlics have slightly bigger, white bulbs of uniform shape and size, with compact cloves that are resistant to pests and diseases.

The 'Jamnagar' garlic is the biggest and the best, ideally suited for garlic powder of good pungency and antibacterial activity.

2. *Creole Garlic*

The Creoles are gorgeous to look at, and are one of the easiest eating raw garlics, owing to a taste that is rich and full, but only very moderate pungency, though Creole Red and Ajo Rajo are noticeably stronger.

This variety retains its flavour well when cooked.

It has eight to 12 cloves per bulb, arranged in a circular configuration.

Both the bulb wrappers and the clove covers have a beautiful vivid rose colour.

They are more tolerant of adverse weather conditions than most garlics.

3. *Purple Stripe Garlic*

This type is usually vividly striped with purplish vertical stripes decorating the bulb wrappers, hence their name.

In between the purple stripes, their bulb wrappers are usually very white and thick.

Some sub-varieties are even heavily splotched with purple.

Colouration is affected by growing conditions, particularly weather, and sometimes they are strongly coloured, and at other times more white than purple.

They tend to be rather rich in flavour, but not overly pungent, though some are milder, and store fairly well.

Standard Purple Stripes—Chesnok Red and Persian Star, make the sweetest roasted garlic.

They mature about midway through the local harvest season, although the larger ones may mature later.

In addition to the Standard Purple Stripe, there are two other groups of Purple Stripe varieties—the glazed group and the marbled group.

Both seem to have thicker bulb wrappers, and fewer cloves per bulb than the standard group.

Purple Stripes can be very beautiful garlics that range from the very strong, such as Metechi or Skuri, or very mild, such as Siberian.

Persian Star and Chesnok Red have a rich medium flavour.

4. *Porcelain*

These garlics are among the most beautiful garlics of all, sometimes too beautiful to eat.

Their bulb wrappers tend to be very thick, luxuriant and parchment-like, and tightly cover their few, but large, cloves.

The outer bulb wrappers are often very white, and tend to have some purple strips as you peel away the wrappers.

Their appearance tempts one to wonder whether they were sculpted by some great artist rather than something grown in the ground.

There are few, or no smaller cloves, as most cloves are large and fat, typically only five really big cloves per bulb.

Porcelains are generally strong-tasting garlics with a few exceptions, and can store up to eight months or more at cool room temperature.

Bulb wrappers vary from white and ivory to very purplish (Romanian Red).

Clove covers have elongated tips, and a golden-brown colour, with some having distinctive, vertical, purplish streaks.

5. *Rocambole*

These garlics tend to have thinner bulb wrappers than other hard-necks, and lots of purple striping and splotches.

They are not as white as other hard necks, and seem to have a brownish cast to them.

In fact, some of them look almost as though they need a bath.

What they lack in beauty, they are said to make up for in taste. Many people consider them their favourite garlics.

In the spring they send up a scape, or stalk, that form a complete double loop.

They have usually six to eight cloves, arranged in circular fashion about a central scape, and have few or no smaller internal cloves.

Apart from these basic groups of hard-necks, the other few are as follows.

The Carpathian Red is a variety that is sturdy and strong.

The Dugansky is a mellow, moderately hot, and long-storing variety.

The German Red is hot-flavoured and tasty, ideal choice for cold-winter regions.

The Spanish Roja are medium-sized cloves that peel easily, and offer medium hot flavour.

The Brown Saxon stays usable longer than most soft-necks.

Soft-neck Garlics

Soft-neck garlics tend to be hotter, and have a narrower range of flavour.

They usually produce larger heads, which last longer in storage.

The soft-neck garlic is the most common and popular variety.

It is the easiest to grow, being very adaptable in a variety of climates and soils.

These types of garlic are productive, and produce smaller cloves per plant than other varieties, and also are very popular for braiding.

The garlic flavour ranges from very mild to very hot, and lack the subtle but more complex flavours of the hard-neck varieties.

Soft-neck garlic can be stored longer than any other type, in fact, up to ten months under optimum conditions.

Two categories of this type includes Artichoke Garlic and Silverskin.

Soft-neck garlics can be spring planted in some regions, with limited success.

Soft-necks generally have about twice as many cloves per bulb as the hard-necks.

While the hard-neck garlics tend to be more colourful, and have fewer, but larger, cloves per bulb than the soft-necks, and a deeper flavour, they don't store as long.

1. *Artichoke Garlic*

This garlic is the kind often seen in most supermarkets in Western countries.

Huge quantities of it are grown in Gilroy (California) and shipped to various countries.

These are easy to grow and seem less fussy about growing conditions than the other varieties.

They have lots of cloves, usually around 12 to 20, with lot of smaller internal cloves.

These garlics store well, and have a wide range of flavours with some, like Simoneti and Red Toch, being very mild and pleasant, and others, such as Inchelium Red and Susanville, have greater depth of flavour.

The Chinese Purple and Purple Cauldron are much stronger, and store well.

The Asiatic types tend to send up scapes, despite the fact that they are soft-necks, and have a little more colour to the bulb wrappers than the main group, which are usually white.

The Turban group of artichoke garlics tend to be the most colourfully artichokes, and have fewer cloves per bulb than the others.

47

The Turbans also harvest earlier, and store less long than the other artichokes, and a good bit stronger in taste as well.

Artichoke garlics are the commercial growers favourite, as they are easier to grow, and produce larger bulbs than most other garlics.

They are also called Red Garlics or Italian Garlics, despite the fact that most are neither red nor were grown in Italy.

The artichoke garlic is named for how the cloves curl up around the core of small cloves just as the leaves of an artichoke curve up around its core.

2. *Silverskin Garlic*

The Silverskin garlics are usually, but not always, the ones that you see in braids.

They are generally the longest storing of all garlics, and have a soft, pliable neck that leads itself to braiding.

They hold up over time better than the artichokes whose necks tend to deteriorate earlier than the silverskins.

They are usually fairly hot and strong garlics, with very few varieties being mild.

Their bulb wrappers are very white, although the clove covers can be strikingly beautiful as in the case of Nootka Rose or Rose du Var.

Silverskins have more cloves per bulb, on the average, than the artichokes, but are nearly not as large.

The Creole group of silverskins are a unique and truly beautiful group of garlics.

The other varieties of soft-neck garlics are as follows-:

Chet's Italian Red is a very mild variety.

Creole Red is good looking and good flavoured. It is one of the top choices in most tastings.

California Early is mild, with a mildly sweet flavour.

California Late is spicy hot.

3. *Elephant Garlic*

This large bulb is really a type of leek, and does not have a very strong garlic flavour.

A large elephant garlic is about twice the size of the largest real garlic.

It has a milder taste, but a sharp onion-like edge to it, and a distinct after-taste.

The elephant garlics average five monstrously large cloves that are somewhat yellowish, compared to the milky real garlic.

It grows extremely clean, and disease-free, and does not seem to be bothered by insects.

4

Composition

Onions

Onions not only provide flavour, they also provide health-promoting petro-chemicals as well as nutrients.

The colour of an onion gives you an insight into its properties.

The white onions are the strongest, followed by the yellow, with red or purple being the mildest-flavoured types.

But there are certain white ones that are juicy and less pungent.

Onions and garlic are rich in powerful sulphur-containing compounds that are responsible for their pungent odours, and for many of their health-promoting effects.

Onions contain allyl propyl disulphide, while garlic is rich in allicin, diallyl disulphide, diallyl trisulphide and others.

In addition, onions are rich in chromium, a trace mineral that helps cells respond to insulin, plus vitamin C, and numerous flavonoids, most notably, quercetin.

In general, the most pungent onions deliver many times the benefits of their milder cousins.

Shallots have the most phenols, six times the amount found in Vidalia onion, the variety with the lowest phenolic content.

They also have the most antioxidant activity.

Yellow onions have the most flavonoids 11 times the amount found in Western while, the variety with the lowest flavonoid content.

For all varieties of onions, the more phenols and flavonoids they contain, the more antioxidant and anti-cancer activity they provide.

When tested against liver and colon cancer cells, yellow shallots were more effective in inhibiting their growth. So next time your eyes water while slicing or peeling onions, be glad, for the onion you are cutting is likely to be loaded with beneficial phytonutrients.

An analysis of the onion shows the following contents:

(i)	moisture:	87 %
(ii)	protein:	1.2 %
(iii)	fibre:	0.6 %
(iv)	minerals:	0.4 %
(v)	carbohydrate:	11.1 %
(vi)	calcium:	47 mg %
(vii)	phosphorus:	50 %
(viii)	iron:	0.7 mg %
(ix)	carotene:	15 mcg %
(x)	riboflavin:	0.01 mg %
(xi)	niacin:	0.4 mg %
(xii)	thiamine:	0.08 mg %

Considered to be the dynamite of natural foods, the onion is relatively high in food value, compared with other vegetables.

It is rich in calcium and riboflavin, while moderate in protein content.

The fresh herb and bulbs yield about 0.005 per cent of an essential oil that has an acrid taste and an unpleasant odour.

Allyl propyl disulphide is the chief component of the crude oil.

Sulphur compounds lend the onion its odour, which is produced only when the layers are cut or injured by enzyme action on the water-soluble amino acid.

When the onion is dried, either by heating or freezing, there is no enzyme action.

When cooking it, there is a different odour, flavour and pungency.

The cooked onions are less smelling and pungent, as compared to the raw ones.

Their smell gets further reduced, if they are roasted under a cover of hot sand. But the cooked or roasted onions lose 10-60 per cent of their vitamin C content.

The raw onion that smells the most is effective antiseptically, is more powerful, and medicinally more preferable.

Being covered by a thin, colourless outer skin, the onions will not emit much smell as such, but when this skin is removed, and the layers are cut, the smell starts emanating.

Onions are low in calories and a good source of vitamin A, especially the green ones.

They also contain ethyl disulphides, vinyl sulphide, and other sulphides and thioles.

The lachrymatory principle is variously identified as thiopropanal-s-oxide, or its tantometer, propenyl sulphenic acid.

Though onions are low in calories, they are also low in most vitamins and minerals.

However, leeks, shallots, scallions, garlic and onions are all rich sources of a number of phytonutrients.

They also contain saponins, which lower the cholesterol and inhibit tumours.

They are high in energy and water content.

They have a generous amount of vitamin B6, vitamin B1, and folic acid.

In his book, *Code of Health and Longevity*, Sir John Sinclair writes, "Onions can never be sufficiently recommended; they possess more nourishment than perhaps any other vegetable. It is a well-known fact a Highlander, with a few onions in his pocket, and a crust of bread or a bit of cake, can work or travel to an almost incredible extent two or three days together without any other sort of food whatsoever. The French are aware of this. The soup, a l'orgnon, is now universally in use after all meetings and dances as the best of all restoratives. Garlics, of all plants, has the greatest strengths, affords more nourishment, and supplies more spirits to those who eat little flesh.

Most of the labourers in rural India use raw onions with rice or roti, which form their staple food.

Garlic

What makes garlic stink? When the garlic cells are ruptured by cutting or pressing, they release an enzyme called allinaise, which chemically changes the inherent alliin to allicin, a sulphur containing molecule. This results in that heady, pungent garlic smell.

These sulphur molecules are absorbed into the bloodstream and lungs, escaping through exhaled air and perspiration.

Thus, the garlic breath in some people, who consume very large quantities of garlic, is very noticeable.

Garlic contains a wealth of sulphur compounds, the most important for taste being allicin, a diallyl disulphide oxide.

This is produced enzymatically from alliin, which is 5-2 propenyl-L-cysteine sulphoxide.

An analysis of garlic per 100 gm shows the following constituents:

(i)	moisture:	62 %
(ii)	protein:	6.3 %
(iii)	fat:	0.1 %
(iv)	minerals:	1%
(v)	fibre:	0.8 %
(vi)	carbohydrates:	29.8 %
(vii)	calcuim:	30 mg %
(viii)	phosphorus:	3.10 mg %
(ix)	iron:	1.3 mg %
(x)	thiamine:	0.06 mg %
(xi)	riboflavin:	0.23 mg %
(xii)	niacin:	0.4 mg %
(xiii)	vitamin C:	13 mg %

Garlic also has traces of iodine, sulphur and chlorine.

It has a strong and characteristic odour and an acrid taste.

It yields an offensively smelling oil, the essence of garlic, identical with allyle sulphide.

When you eat the garlic, this odour is evolved by the excretory organs, the activity of which it promotes.

When eaten in great quantities, garlic may be strongly evident in the diner's sweat the following day.

The bulb yields an essential oil containing allyl propyl trisulphide, diallyl disulphide, diallyl trisulphide, diallyl sulphide, ajeone, and minor amounts of polysulphides.

Sulphur compounds of this kind are typical of the onion family.

This oil is a clear, limpid liquid, dark brown or yellowish in colour.

It can be purified or distilled without any decomposition whatsoever.

The freshly extracted juice from garlic is rich in the oil, and consists of an abundant amount of bound sulphur (that is, organic sulphides), and iodine and salic acid combinations, apart from important nutrient and complementary substances containing vitamins.

Allacin is another active substance extracted from garlic. This has now been tested to be beneficial against various disease-causing micro-organisms.

Garlic also contains antiseptic and hypotensive principals, known as allicin, allisation I and allisation II. They are useful in lowering high blood pressure and blood cholesterol.

In some places in France, people eat garlic with fresh butter every day in the spring season, and this, they believe, keeps them healthy and energetic all the year round.

5

Selection and Storage

Onions

Onions are a major source of the photonutrients, phenols and flavonoids, that are known to be protective against cancer and cardiovascular diseases.

A research study published in the *Journal of Agricultural and Food Chemistry* (November 2004 issue) shows that the variety of onions you chose, and the way you prepare them make a vast difference in the amount of beneficial compounds, and the antioxidant and antiseptic effects that they deliver.

Selection

Choose onions that are clean, well-shaped, have no opening at the neck, and have crisp, dry outer skins.

Look for those that feel dry and solid all over, with no soft spots. The neck should be slightly closed.

The outer skin should have a crackly feel and a shiny appearance.

Avoid those that are sprouting, or have signs of mould.

Onions of inferior quality often have soft spots, moisture at their neck, and dark patches, which may all be indications of decay.

As conventionally grown onions are often irradiated to prevent them from sprouting, purchase organically grown varieties, as they are not treated with this process.

Avoid selecting onions with green areas or dark patches. They should smell mild, even if their flavour is not.

As a rule, the large, mild spring and summer onions should be ideal for eating raw, or for cooked dishes in which you want a subtle flavour.

The crisp, assertive character of storage onions makes them better suited for dishes that require long cooking, since they can hold their flavour.

An onion's flavour is determined by its variety, and also by the soil and climatic conditions where it grows. Consequently onions with the same appearance can taste considerably different, depending on where and when they were grown.

So, you have to experiment, particularly when it comes to choosing the mildest onions.

Several people prefer a particular colour of onions, though colour is not a reliable guide to flavour or texture.

White onions tend to be more pungent than yellow or red, but this rule of thumb may not be true in your locality.

Size is another consideration. For raw onion slices in salads and sandwiches, select large ones.

They are also a more efficient choice for peeling and chopping.

For cooking whole or in chunks, choose small to medium-sized ones.

When purchasing scallions or leeks, look for those that have green, fresh looking tops which appear crisp, yet tender.

The base should be whitish in colour for two or three inches.

Avoid those that have wilted or yellow tops. Onions with pointed ends last longer, and are easier to chop.

Storage

Onions should be stored at room temperature, away from bright light, which can turn their flavour better.

They do best in an area that allows plenty of air to circulate around them.

To do this, spread them out in a single layer, or place them in a wire hanging basket, or a perforated bowl with a raised base, so that there is ventilation from all sides.

Since onions absorb moisture, causing them to spoil more quickly, avoid storing them under a sink.

Avoid placing them near potatoes which give off moisture, and produce ethylene gas that causes onions to spoil more quickly. High humidity too will considerably reduce storage time.

If an onion begins to sprout, use it quickly, since it has probably started to turn mushy.

The length of the storage varies with the type of onion stored.

Those that are pungent in flavour, such as yellow ones, can stay longer than those with a sweeter taste, such as white onions, since the compounds that confer their sharp taste help to preserve them.

Scallions should be stored in a perforated plastic bag in the refrigerator where they will keep for a week.

Cut onions should be wrapped tightly in plastic or in a sealed container, consumed within a day or two since they tend to oxidise and lose their nutrient content rather quickly.

Cooked onions, tightly covered in glass or plastic containers can be stored in the refrigerator for five days or so. They should never be placed in a metal container as this may cause them to discolour.

Garlic

Selection

For maximum flavour and nutritional benefits, always purchase fresh garlic.

Although garlic, in the form of flakes, powder or paste, may be more convenient, you will derive less culinary and health benefits from these forms.

Purchase garlic that is plump, and has an unbroken skin.

Gently squeeze the garlic bulb between your fingers to check that it feels firm, and is not damp.

Avoid garlic that is soft, mouldy, shrivelled, or that has begun to sprout, These may be indications of decay that will cause the flavour and texture to be inferior.

Size is not often an indication of quality.

If your recipe calls for a large amount of garlic, remember that it is always easier to peel and chop a few larger ones.

While buying garlic, ensure that the heads are firm to the touch, with no nicks on soft cloves.

If you notice dark, powdery patches under the skin, pass it up since it is an indication of a common mould which will eventually spoil the flesh.

Garlic heads that are heavy and compact are mostly the best selection. Reject the light ones.

Storage

Store fresh garlic in either an uncovered, or a loosely covered, container in a cool, dark place, away from exposure to heat and sunlight. This will help maintain its maximum freshness, and help prevent sprouting.

When garlic starts sprouting, its flavour gets reduced, and the pod shrivels.

It is not necessary to refrigerate garlic.

Some people freeze peeled garlic. However, this process reduces its flavour and changes its texture.

Depending upon its age and variety, whole garlic bulbs will keep fresh for up to two months.

Inspect the bulb frequently, and remove any cloves that appear to be dried out or mouldy.

Once you break the head of garlic, it greatly reduces its shelf life to just a few days.

Garlic can also be purchased as peeled whole cloves, or in the form of a paste.

In some countries, they are minced and stored in oil.

It is imperative that garlic in oil be stored under refrigeration to avoid potentially-deadly bacteria growth.

If you use a lot of garlic, and wish to cut your preparation time down, you can also pre-peel and store them in oil.

But the best flavour comes from freshly peeled cloves.

Use garlic powder, garlic salt and garlic extract or juice only as a last resort.

If you crush the garlic, use it within a day, as it is likely to spoil.

Otherwise, grind it with an equal quantity of salt, and store in the refrigerator. This can stay for a year.

While using it for cooking, use this garlic salt instead of the regular salt.

Don't discard garlic cloves that have become discoloured. Roast them gently in a pan over a low flame. When cool, powder it and store in an airtight container.

6

Benefits in Cuisines

Onions

Onion is an ingredient in a number of recipes, from the main course to soups and salads, dips and curries.

They are used in breakfast, lunch, dinner, bread, snacks, etc.

They may be eaten raw or cooked.

They should be peeled before preparing, except while baking.

They may be boiled, fried, baked, braised, microwaved or sautéed.

They can be sliced, chopped, diced, grated or ground, but first they must be peeled.

Peeling and Cutting

To make the task of peeling easier, especially if you need to prepare a large quantity of onions, trim off the tops and bottoms, and place the onions in boiling water for about a minute. Drain the water, and pull off the outer skin which would be loose. Now you can chop or slice it.

With small, white boiling onions, cut a cross in the root end of each one, which keeps the onion intact once you slip off the outer skin.

While many people love to eat onions most dread cutting them since this process usually brings tears to the eyes.

The compound that causes the eyes to smart is a phytochemical known as allyl sulphate that is produced when sulphur compounds released by the onion's ruptured cells are exposed to air.

If cutting onion irritates your eyes, a few tricks should be employed. Chill the onions for an hour before cutting them. This will slow down the activity of the enzyme that produces the allyl sulphate, and is a better choice than the traditional method of cutting onion under running water which may dilute the amount of allyl sulphate that is responsible for significant health benefits.

Use a very sharp knife, and always cut the onions while standing; that way your eyes will be as far away as possible.

You may also consider wearing glasses or goggles.

Cut off the top, but leave the root on, as this has the largest amount of sulphur compounds, which is what causes tears when the onion is peeled or cut.

Remove the root prior to cooking or eating.

If you need to grind the onions for gravy, cut them into halves, and boil in a pressure cooker. Grind the boiled onions, and sautée the paste.

Cut the onions into halves, and leave them for a few minutes before you chop them finely. This way there will be less tears.

You can even try this—chew a gum while peeling onions. Your eyes will be dry!

To prevent onion tears, bite and hold a safety pin between your teeth while chopping the onions.

Use Onions Daily

Make onions part of your every day meal.

Use raw or cooked onions to season curries, stews, soups, sauces, gravies, etc.

Enjoy them on their own, stuffed and baked.

Stuff them with chopped vegetables and rice or breadcrumbs.

Add raw onions to salads, to add crunch and flavour to dressings, relishes or sauces.

Cooking Methods

Although some recipes call for raw onions to be cooked with other ingredients, others require them to be cooked beforehand.

Virtually every cooking method has been used with onions.

Since they are low in minerals, the length of cooking time should be minimal.

Prolonged cooking takes away the flavour out of onions. Cook only until they are tender.

Baking

When you bake the onions, use them whole, without removing the outer skin.

71

Cut off the root ends, so that the onions will stand upright in the baking pan. Prick them with a fork, and place in the baking pan, lightly coated with a little oil or nonstick spray.

Or peel them, pierce them, and then wrap them in foil. Bake them whole.

Boiling

Boiling is best for whole and half onions, but also works for sliced onions. These are good for making sambars.

Braising

Small, white, pearl onions, or Madras onions that are small and red, can be braised by placing them in a pan filled with half-inch water. Cover and simmer over low heat until the liquid is absorbed, and the onions are tender.

Microwave

To microwave onions, place the cut onions in a microwaveable casserole dish, add two tablespoons of water, and cook for seven to eight minutes.

Sauté

Sautéing can be done in oil on a low heat, stirring constantly.

Frying

By frying, onions change their taste, turning sweeter and more aromatic. Long after frying in comparatively cool oil, the flavour develops.

In Central Europe, fried onion rings are popularly used for decorating or garnishing dishes, like the German potatoes.

Even in Indonesia and Vietnam, the fried onion rings are used to top their fried rice.

These fried rings remain crisp if stored in an airtight container.

Onion Pastes

Many people prepare pastes of onions by grinding the onions together with a variety of spices.

Since raw onions easily turn bitter on long storage, such pastes are better prepared fresh and used immediately.

Alternatively, they can be preserved by adding vinegar or lemon juice.

In India, most people fry the paste in oil which keeps for 2-3 days without spoiling.

Indonesia displays a great variety of onion-based spice pastes.

73

From the New World, Jamaica Jerk is the most famous example of onion based paste, used mainly to marinate meat or fish.

Gravies

In India, nearly every North Indian and Mughlai recipe calls for onions in their sauces and gravies. The chopped onions are fried along with fresh garlic and ginger, and dried spices like red chillies, coriander seeds, cuminseeds, black cardamom, turmeric, etc. These are then pureed, and simmered with tomatoes or curds, or added to boiling vegetables or meat.

Indian cooking is an art, for the error of adding too much or too little of this spiced masala becomes manifest only in the last phase of cooking, when corrections are difficult to make.

In Mughlai cuisine, cinnamon, bay leaves and cloves are an addition to the wet masala, and used most lavishly at the cost of pungent chillies.

In Myanmar, their cuisine is a blend of Chinese, Indian and Thai gravies, giving it a unique taste. Their meat cubes or vegetables are braised in a rich, spicy gravy that contains onions, vinegar, fresh garlic and ginger, cuminseeds, coriander, and of course, chillies. This gravy is fried in sesame oil until the fat separates from the gravy. This long frying lends it that unique and complex taste.

Dried Onion

In many countries in the West, onions are dried, in which case they again change their flavour, and turn more garlic-like.

In the southern states of America and in Mexico, dried onion forms part of the commercially available chile-con-carne spice mixtures, together with cuminseed, oregano, garlic, pepper and chillies.

Shallots

Shallots are more popular in northern France, where they are essential for sauces based on red wine. They are not fried, but mostly cooked or braised, as in their sauce bearnaise.

Raw Onions

A very beneficial way of eating onions is to eat them raw.

Chop the onions, garnish with a little lemon juice, black pepper and a little chopped chillies. This ensures the greatest amount of juice and vitamins.

You can chop the onions finely, soak them in buttermilk, wash and then cook to remove their odour without loss of vitamins.

Browning Onions

To speed up the browning of fried onions, add a trace of sugar or table salt.

If you keep the chopped onions in sunlight for an hour and then fry them, they will consume less oil.

Alternatively, roast the chopped onions in hot pan for a few seconds, and then add the oil for frying. This makes the onion brown faster, and you will save on oil also.

Another way to make them brown and crisp is to add a pinch of maida to the oil before removing the fried onions from the oil.

Garlic

Garlic is one of the most versatile flavours to grace a kitchen.

It not only tastes wonderful, it is very good for your body—a precious gift to cooks of all levels of expertise.

Peeling Garlics

To peel garlic flakes easily and quickly, add a teaspoon of oil to about 200 gms of garlic cloves, and keep in the sunlight for 10-15 minutes.

Another way to peel the garlic is to cut it lengthwise, and then peel it. This way the skin gets removed faster.

Place the garlic pods on the lid of a hot pressure cooker, or any lid covering a hot dish. After 15 minutes, when you peel the cloves, the skin comes off easily.

Soak the cloves of garlic in a little water before peeling. The skin will come off easily, and you will not hurt your nails.

Place the garlic pod in the oven for a minute. You can peel them with ease.

Pods of garlic can be easily peeled by warming them in a dry pan.

Cooking Methods

Garlic Flavour

One raw garlic clove, finely minced or pressed, releases more flavour than a dozen cooked whole cloves.

When garlic cloves are cooked or baked whole, the flavour mellows into a sweet, almost nutty flavour that is devoid of pungency.

While sautéing garlic, be sure not to burn it as the flavour then turns intensely bitter.

It is well to remember that the small you chop the cloves, the stronger will be the flavour.

Raw Garlic

Some cuisines are fond of raw garlic. In some parts of Austria, minced garlic is combined with vinegar, salad oil and salt for salads.

Mediterranean sauces use a lot of raw garlic, for example, the Provencal speciality called aioli, a mayonnaise prepared with olive oil and enriched with raw garlic paste.

The Greek skordalia is a paste made from cooked potatoes and raw garlic.

The Turkish cacik is a refreshing soup made from plain curds, shredded cucumber, garlic and peppermint leaves.

A thicker saucey product, known as tsatsiki in Greek, is served with barbecued lamb. Sauces make use of a lot of raw garlic mince.

In West Asia, many appetisers contain fresh garlic.

You may occasionally see minced garlic spread along the edges of an Italian pizza.

In northern Vietnam, freshly grated garlic is served in liberal amounts to spring rolls and soups, especially the Hanoi style beef soup.

The latter is an example demonstrating the subtle effect that can be achieved by adding grated or squeezed raw garlic to a dish that already contains cooked garlic.

Pickled Garlic

You can pickle garlic in vinegar, olive oil or sesame oil. Since some of the garlic's aroma is extracted by the liquid, pickled garlic is usually mild.

Fried Garlic

The more common usage of garlic is frying it. On heating, the pungency and strong odour gets lost, and the aroma becomes more subtle and less dominant, harmonising perfectly with ginger, pepper, chillies and other spices. Therefore, it is an essential ingredient for nearly every cuisine of the world.

Asian cuisines make different use of this very versatile spice. Garlic is added in an early phase in many Indian recipes.

In contrast, the Indonesian and Chinese stir-fries usually start with frying a few cloves of garlic, but a faint garlic aroma persists until serving because of the much shorter cooking time.

The Indonesians marinate the meat pieces with a mixture based on minced garlic, ginger and chillies before roasting or grilling.

Garlic Paste

Thai cuisine prefers gentle simmering for spicy soups or creamy curries, thereby avoiding frying of garlics.

In Cambodia too, pastes of garlic, lemon grass, chillies and ginger are added to the boiling soups or stews.

Garlic Powder

Garlic powder is used in marinades, or mixed with herbs, and rubbed into pork, beef or poultry before cooking.

When you add a few cloves of garlic or some garlic powder to the fat in the roasting tin while it is hot in the oven, it delicately flavours the fat and the joint. You must make sure that the garlic cloves (or powder) are under the joint.

7

Health Benefits

Onions and garlic contain natural chemicals that can have powerful health-boosting effects on the body. The health benefits of eating onions and garlic on a daily basis were well known to our ancestors. They used them to protect themselves from illnesses, and to act as an antiseptic for a wide range of infections.

Modern dietary advice, supported by scientific evidence, emphasises the benefits of a daily intake of onions and garlic.

These pungent, natural foods contain chemicals that can protect the body from so many major and minor illnesses, including cardiovascular disease, infections, diabetes, respiratory problems, cancers, etc.

Work them into your daily diet by eating them raw (ideally) or cooked. Use them to flavour food.

Crush, mince or chop them, and use them in as many ordinary day-to-day recipes as you can.

Don't just think of them as occasional food items to be used for special meals, or when entertaining.

Allow your imagination to come up with new ways of incorporating them into your daily diet—ideas that will suit you and fit in with your family preferences.

Onions

Onion was reputed to cure virtually all diseases in ancient days.

The physicians in ancient Egypt and Mesopotamia prescribed onions to cure various diseases.

Many herbal remedies were attributed to onions by Dioscorides in first century AD.

Onion is highly valued for its therapeutic properties.

To get the best for curing these diseases it is advisable to use onion juice instead of the whole onion.

In a nutshell, the following are the main benefits derived from onions-:

1. It boosts good type HDL cholesterol (especially when consumed raw).
2. It reduces total cholesterol levels.
3. It increases blood-clot dissolving activity.
4. It reduces the risk of diabetes.
5. It attacks bacteria that causes infection.
6. It reduces the risk of certain cancers.

Onions contain chemicals that help fight the free radicals in our bodies. These free radicals cause disease and destruction to cells which are linked to at least 60 diseases.

The leaves of the plant are digestive, diuretic, carminative, expectorant, anti-spasmodic, aphrodisiac, tonic, emollient, stimulant and mild laxative.

Onions are useful in the treatment of the following ailments.

Acidity

Eating white chopped onions mixed with curds and a little sugar relieves one of the burning sensation due to acidity in the stomach.

It will also mitigate the disorders that arise due to the aggravation of bile.

Anaemia

Eating daily a pickle made of onion, salt, black pepper and chopped radish is beneficial in treating anaemia and nausea.

Arteriosclerosis

Onions have a specific effect in arteriosclerosis. They are especially rich in organic silicon which keeps the blood at a normal temperature.

Arthritis

Several anti-inflammatory agents in onions render them helpful in reducing the severity of symptoms associated with inflammatory conditions such as the pain and swelling of osteoarthritis and rheumatoid arthritis.

Onions possess pain-killing properties, and are beneficial in the treatment of pain due to arthritis.

The regular use of onions, especially in the raw form, can help reduce inflammation.

Ascitis

Medication of onion is advantageous in the case of ascitis in which there is a collection of morbid fluid in the belly, and therefore its consequential bloating.

Asthma

Onions possess anti-inflammatory agents that reduce the allergic inflammatory response of asthma.

Eating raw onions twice or thrice a day gives relief to patients of asthma, nasal and bronchial catarrh.

Atherosclerosis

Onions have a specific effect in atherosclerosis, and is therefore useful as a prophylaxis in cardiovascular disorders.

Bacterial Infections

Raw onions are great for killing harmful bacteria in the mouth.

Blood Clot

Since onions have coagulant properties, eating them either in raw or cooked form helps keep the blood free of clots, partly because their compounds hinder platelet clumping, and increases clot-dissolving activity.

Onions are known to thin the blood, thereby reducing its tendency to form blood clots within the arteries.

Blood Disorders

The seeds of onion are known to purify the blood.

Boils

Roasted onions, used as a poultice to indolent boils, help them to mature and burst faster. Thus it is considered to be a very good cosmetic agent.

Cancer

Onions are rich in a flavonoid called quercetin that is a potent antioxidant, and been linked to protection from several diseases, including cancer.

They have been ranked on their ability to fight cancer, and if you value your health more than fresh breath, take note—the stinky ones win out.

When it comes to onions' cancer-fighting abilities, the stinker the better.

Amongst onions, those with the strongest flavours have the highest antioxidant activity, and are best for inhibiting the growth of liver and colon cancer cells.

Certain research studies show that people who are more health-conscious might want to go with the stronger onions rather than the mild ones.

The regular use of onions, as little as two of more times per week, is associated with a significantly reduced risk of developing colon cancers.

Onions are far better at inhibiting the growth of colon cancer cells than liver cancer cells (though they are useful in both), suggesting that they are better colon fighters.

The flavonoid quercetin is known to protect colon cells from the damaging effects of certain cancer-causing substances.

Cooking meats with onions may help reduce the amount of carcinogen's produced when meat is cooked in certain ways.

While cooking can reduce the nutritional value of some foods, it has been shown to increase the cancer-fighting ability of others, such as those containing lycopene.

Onions and garlic are both antioxidants that are beneficial to ones health. The healing power of onions is due to the natural antioxidant, quercetin, which neutralises free radicals that can damage the cell and harm DNA.

Early research links the antioxidant to preventing the development of cancer cells.

Children's Ailments

For chronic stomach pains in children, give them onion juice extracted from baked onions.

For treating dysentery in children, burn a peepal stick and extinguish it in onion juice. Mix the juice well and administer it to the child. The dysentery will soon cease.

The juice from a baked onion can also be used as an effective ear drop to mitigate earache in children.

If children have pain in the eyes, mix the juice from a baked onion with an equal quantity of pure honey and a little rosewater. One or two drops of this in the eyes twice a day proves beneficial.

Cholera

Onion is also known to be an effective remedy for cholera.

Given with black pepper to patients of cholera, it helps in allaying thirst and feelings of restlessness, and the patient feels better.

It also mitigates the effects of nausea and diarrhoea.

When cholera is epidemic in one's area, onions should be cut into pieces and spread all around the house to prevent an attack of the disease.

Eating a lot of onions with salt during such an epidemic can help prevent the infection.

Onion juice mixed with lime juice also helps in controlling the spasms and convulsions of the body during the cholera infection.

Cardiovascular Disorders

Onions, tea, apples and broccoli are the richest sources of flavonoids, and people consuming them regularly are at a very low risk of a heart disease.

The presence of essential oil, allyl propyl disulphide, catechol, protocatechnic acid, thiopropiono aldehyde, thiocyanate and vitamins in onions help in preventing caradiovascular disease.

Shallots and onion varieties with the strongest flavour have the highest total antioxidant activity, an indication that they have a stronger ability to destroy charged molecules, called free radicals, an excess of which increases the risk of cancer.

Cholesterol Control

The regular consumption of onions has shown to lower high cholesterol levels preventing atherosclerosis and diabetic heart disease, as also reducing the risk of a heart attack or stroke.

One teaspoon of raw onion juice early in the morning is said to be excellent for heart problems and blood cholesterol.

According to Dr. Victor Gurewich, a cardiologist and professor of medicine at Harvard Medical School, half a raw onion, or equivalent in juice, raises the HDL an average 30 per cent in most people with cholesterol problems.

Onions are largely responsible for normalising percentages of blood cholesterol by oxidising the excess cholesterol.

Adenosine, another chemical found in the onions, is linked to thinning the blood, and lowering LDL cholesterol.

Although eating onions raw works better to thin the blood and increase circulation, cooking them will not destroy these healthful chemicals.

Cold and Cough
Quercetin and other flavonoids work with vitamin C to help kill harmful bacteria, making onions especially good addition to soups and stews during cold and flu season.

The anti-inflammatory agents in onions reduce the severity of the respiratory congestion associated with common cold.

The quercetin found in the onion has anti-viral and anti-bacterial activity, and hence is most beneficial in the treatment of several viral diseases, including cold and influenza.

Consuming a hot roasted onion before retiring to bed at night is an effective remedy for common cold.

Drinking the water in which onions have been boiled till the water has reduced by half, reduces the suffering of consumptive coughing.

Onion juice with honey is beneficial in the treatment of common cold, chronic bronchitis, or inflammation of the bronchi or wind pipe.

Constipation

Three medium-sized onions, ground with a fistful of tender tamarind leaves, and eaten in the form of a chutney, relieves constipation problems.

Dental Disorders

Onion is useful in treating both tooth and gum disorders.

Eating a raw onion every day protects the teeth from a host of disorders.

Dr. B.P. Tohkin, a Russian dentist, claims that chewing raw onion for three minutes is enough to kill all the germs in the mouth.

A small piece of onion placed on a bad tooth allays toothache.

Chewing it with salt gives relief from inflammation of the gums, by destroying the germs in the gums.

The virulently pungent and the smarting volatile oil found in the onion bulb is of benefit to those who have spongy gums caused due to lack of vitamin C.

For nicotine poisoning, administering two teaspoons of onion juice will be immediately beneficial.

Diabetes

The higher the intake of onions, the lower the level of glucose found during oral or intravenous glucose tolerance tests.

Experimental and clinical evidence suggests that allyl propyl disulphide is responsible for this effect, and lowers blood sugar levels by increasing the amount of free insulin available.

Allyl propyl disulphide does this by competing with insulin, which is also a disulphide, to occupy the sites in the liver where insulin is inactivated. This results in an increase in the amount of insulin available to usher glucose into cells, causing a lowering of blood sugar.

Onions are also a very good source of chromium, the mineral component in glucose tolerance factor, a molecule that helps cells respond appropriately to insulin.

Clinical studies of diabetes have shown that chromium can decrease blood glucose levels, improves glucose tolerance, total cholesterol and triglyceride levels, while increasing good H DL cholesterol levels.

Onion taken regularly is said to lower blood sugar in diabetes.

Onions have been used since ancient times in the treatment of diabetes.

Research conducted in various universities show that the onions affect the liver's metabolism of glucose, or release of insulins or prevent insulin's destruction.

Allyl propyl disulphide and allicin are the active hypoglycaenic substances in onions which lower the blood sugar.

In 1960, scientists were able to isolate the anti-diabetic compounds from onions. These compounds are similar to the common anti-diabetic pharmaceuticals which help in releasing and stimulating insulin activity.

Digestive Disorders

The volatile oil in the onion confers an appreciable benefit in the colic or shooting pains in the stomach, caused by indigestion.

Eaten raw, onions are natural stimulants and digestives. For people who have poor digestive power, onion cooked with vinegar, and eaten, brings relief.

Dysentery

Onion juice mixed with curds and taken thrice a day stops dysentery and diarrhoea.

Ear Disorders

Onion juice can be used beneficially in the treatment of abscess in the ear caused by middle-ear infection.

Use slightly warm juice in the ear, thrice daily. The effect can be enhanced by adding equal proportions of vinegar and rose water to the juice.

Eczema

To get rid of severe itching, or even eczema, onions should be ground and mixed with wine. Applied on the skin, the itching stops, and the spots disappear gradually.

Epilepsy

For persons prone to epileptic fits, onion juice, drunk daily, acts as a prophylactic measure.

In children prone to frequent fits of epilepsy, white onion is split, and its fresh bit is repeatedly kept in the nostril, or is made to be smelt. This helps to ward off an attack.

Eye Disorders

The quercetin in onions protects against cataracts, apart from heart diseases and cancer.

In the early stages of cataract, use a mixture of onion juice, pure honey and camphor as a colyrium at night before going to bed. This will stop the cataract from spreading.

Fevers

Onion juice is advantageously utilised in the cases of various types of fevers.

Flatulence

Flatulence can be cured by taking onion juice mixed with a pinch of powdered asafoetida (*heeng*) and a pinch of salt every day.

Goitre

In cases of goitre, onion is ground very fine, and applied over the throat. Or else, chopped onions are fried in ghee, and massaged on the throat.

Hair Disorders

Onion juice mixed with honey, and applied frequently on the hair, and massaged into the scalp, may be allowed to soak for an hour. Then wash it off. This prevents excessive hair loss.

This treatment will also promote hair growth, and make the hair roots firm, and the hair dense.

Heart Disease

The sulphur compounds, chromium and vitamin B6, found in onions help prevent heart disease by lowering the high homocysteine levels, another risk factor for heart attack and stroke.

Hiccup

Inhaling the steam from the water, in which onions have been boiled, reduces the severity of hiccups.

Hoarseness

Onion juice cures hoarseness of voice, if taken daily.

Hypertension

The regular consumption of onions has shown to lower high blood pressure thus preventing atherosclerosis and diabetic heart disease, as also reducing the risk of a heart attack.

Inflammation

Onions contain compounds that inhibit lipoxygenase and cyclooxygenase (the enzymes that generate inflammatory prostaglandins and thromboxanes), thus in a marked manner reducing inflammation.

Onions' anti-inflammatory effects are due not only to their vitamin C and quercetin, but to other active components called isothiocyanates.

These compounds work synergistically to give relief from inflammation.

Influenza

Equal amounts of onion juice and honey taken daily, at least three teaspoons, help in combating influenza.

Dr. Melamet, a French military physician during World War II, treated influenza patients at his hospital by giving them the juice of onion in a warm infusion thrice a day.

Even keeping a cut onion in the bedroom is said to prevent the infection of cold and cough during a flu attack.

Eating raw onions thrice a day helps to clear stuffy nostrils resulting from cold.

Insomnia

Onions are good for nerves and insomnia. Consuming raw onion daily purifies the blood and induces sound sleep.

As a cure for sleeplessness, a particularly strong-smelling onion is tied behind the neck of the patient.

A tea or cold infusion of onion seeds, taken twice daily, gives one a sound sleep at night.

Jaundice

For people who have jaundice, onion cooked with vinegar and eaten daily brings relief.

Juice of white onion mixed with jaggery and turmeric powder, and consumed twice a day, is useful in jaundice.

Menstrual Disorders

Onion is a valuable remedy for painful menstruation.

Boil 50 grammes of onion in two litres of water, and allow the water to reduce by half. Cool and drink this thrice daily.

In cases where menstruation does not occur, or there is amenorrhoea, onion juice taken with a little jaggery will set it right.

Neurogenic Pains

People suffering from neurogenic pains anywhere in the body can find relief by tying of poultices of crushed onions in a banana leaf, and warming it slightly before application at bed time. There will be a perceptible relief the next morning.

Nose Bleed

For a bleeding nose, smell the juice of an onion, or use as a nasal drug.

Harita, a celebrated author on ayurveda, recommends the fresh juice extracted from the leaves of the onion to be the best remedy for nose bleed.

The milky white onion is best in preventing bleeding in any haemorrhage.

Taken in soup, curry or gruel, it is very beneficial in cases of extensive haemorrhage, especially for nose bleed.

Osteoporosis

Onions are known to prevent brittle bones. Onions, garlic and a range of other salads may help reduce the risk of osteoporosis, the crippling bone disease that affects one in three women, usually after menopause.

The researchers at the University of Bern in Switzerland say that an onion a day can help prevent the process that causes the condition, the resorption, where calcium seeps from the bones, making them brittle.

Inclusion of onions and garlic in the daily diet could therefore be an effective and inexpensive way to decrease the incidence of osteoporosis.

Pimples

For pimples and eruptions, onion fried in ghee and applied on them is beneficial.

Piles

Onions are useful in suppressing pain, resulting from piles. Occasionally, when piles cause excruciating pain, making it difficult for the patient even to sit, onions give relief. They are baked with their skins, then ground into a paste which is fried in a little ghee. While still hot, the paste is placed on the piles, and a suitable dressing applied. This soothes the pain.

Eating onions fried with caraway seeds in ghee, and mixed with sugar candy, proves beneficial to those suffering from bleeding piles.

An ointment made of onion, turmeric and Indian hemp in hot gingelly oil makes an effective application over pile masses.

Slice an onion, wash and eat it, mixed with curds, once or twice a day for a week, for the treatment of long-standing bleeding piles.

The use of onions is attended by a wholesome effect in the pile-affected patients, and also the prolapse of the rectum.

For the haemorrhoids of the piles, onion seeds are ground with salt and applied on them.

It is also a practice, sometimes adopted, when the haemorrhoid growth of the piles are subjected to a fumigation from the seeds of leek.

Poisonous Bites
Poisonous bites can be treated by applying onion juice mixed with honey.

Also take orally a mixture of onion paste, black pepper powder and cumin powder. Onion soup, taken frequently, also helps.

Application of onion paste mixed with alum also heals stings by wasps and honey bees, or beetles.

For bites by centipedes, onion and garlic pastes mixed together and applied on the bites brings quick relief.

It is also believed that sprinkling onion water in and around the house repels poisonous creatures such as scorpions and snakes.

Respiratory Disorders

Taking onion juice mixed with honey is one of the safest medicines against respiratory disorders. It liquifies phlegm, and prevents its formation.

Phlegmatic complaints, not accompanied with fever, respond very well for a medication with onion, in the aged as well as children.

Onions seeds are also known to expel phlegm from the body.

Rheumatism

Onion juice mixed with mustard oil in equal quantity is applied externally to painful joints with beneficial results, to allay pains and swellings in rheumatic affections.

Sexual Disability

Onions are known to have aphrodisiac properties since prehistoric times.

Sheikh Al Nefzawi, in his book. *The Perfumed Garden,* recommends the use of onion juice mixed with honey to improve sexual power.

Being very potent, onions were forbidden for use by Egyptian priests in olden days.

Onion is believed to increase libido, and strengthen the reproductive organ.

In olden days in France, newly-weds consumed onion soup in the morning after their wedding night, to restore their libido.

Onion with honey is said to be one of the best aphrodisiac foods.

The white one is preferable to the red one for juice, taken with ghee, and chased down with a cup of milk, is said to cure impotency.

Onion seeds too are quite aphrodisiac in nature.

Skin Disorders

Since onions have anti-bacterial and anti-fungal properties, they are useful in treating some skin diseases, like age-old spots, warts or freckles. Onion juice is mixed with vinegar and rubbed gently on the affected areas. This helps in stimulating the circulation of blood in the mucous membrane.

The effect of onion on the diseases of the skin has been seen to be more potent and beneficial than even the calcium sulphide that is usually recommended for this purpose.

In cases of scabies, freckles and discolouring spots on the skin, the onion seeds are ground into a paste and applied.

For ringworm and mole that are particularly thick and black, the seeds are ground to a paste, mixed with vinegar, and applied.

Spleen Enlargement

Onion cooked with vinegar and consumed proves beneficial for those who have spleen enlargement.

Eating daily a pickle made of onion, first soaked in hot salty water, then mixed with salt, black pepper and radish pieces, helps in cases of spleen enlargement.

Sunstroke

To prevent sunstroke, it is advisable to include onions in all the meals.

Swooning

If a person swoons, hold a crushed onion near his nostrils. He will immediately regain consciousness.

Onion juice can also be administered drop by drop into the nostrils to revive him.

Urinary Disorders

Onion, an effective diuretic food is very beneficial in the treatment of urinary disorders.

A decoction of onion is useful in mitigating the burning sensation and micturition during an urinary infection.

For those having scanty urination onions should be boiled in water with a little sugar, and taken frequently. The effect will be compounded if a little potassium nitrate is added to this mixture.

The seeds of onion too are useful in the treatment of urinary disorders, as they have properties to kill bacteria, and bring about excessive urination.

Conclusion

A few points can be highlighted in a nutshell:
1. Eating a raw onion every day is said to keep heart problems away.

2. To stop bleeding a fine paste of onion is applied to the affected area and the bleeding is controlled quickly.

3. Eating onion, which is slightly burnt on the flame, relieves indigestion, and helps control dysentery.

4. Crush a raw onion, and apply the juice from it on the area where a scorpion or bee has stung. The pain will disappear very fast.

5. Crush and extract juice from white raw onions. Add a little turmeric, and apply in areas where you have eczema.

6. Onion eaten raw with a piece of jaggery helps purify the blood and also helps in gaining weight.

7. Eating raw onions every day, not only induce sound sleep, but also activate the nervous system.

Garlic

Besides the mythical acclaim for warding off vampires and other evil spirits, garlic has a centuries-old reputation for its health and healing qualities.

Today this plant ranks as our most popular herbal cure-all. And it may indeed have some untapped medicinal potential.

Pliny, the Roman writer gives an exceedingly long list of complaints in which garlic was considered to be beneficial.

Dr. T. Sydenham valued it as an application in confluent smallpox. Cullen found some dropsies cured by it alone.

Early in the twentieth century it was sometimes used in the treatment of pulmonary tuberculosis.

Garlic has long been considered a medicinal food, being used to protect against plague by monks of the Middle Ages.

It is rich in a variety of powerful sulphur-containing compounds, including thiosulphinates (of which the best known is alliin) and dithiins (in which the most researched compound is ajoene). While these compounds are responsible for garlic's characteristically pungent odour, they are also the source of many of its health promoting effects.

Arthritis
Garlic contains compounds that inhibit the enzymes (which generate inflammatory conditions), thus in a significant manner reducing inflammation.

The anti-inflammatory enzymes contained in garlic are cyclooxygenase and lipoxygenase, which along with vitamin C help in reducing the pain and inflammation of osteoarthritis and rheumatoid arthritis.

Research by physicians in India reveal that garlic eaters often get relief from joint pain, in particular, those with osteoarthritis, which also involves inflammation.

A decoction of garlic taken orally is also beneficial to arthritic patients.

Asthma

The enzymes, lipoxygenase and cyclooxygenase, protect against severe attacks of asthma.

In ancient times, Egyptians and Romans, and in medieval times, Arabs and Persians, used garlic in the treatment of asthma.

Garlic pods boiled in water was administered to the patients, whereby the prostaglandins in the body were affected.

In Cambodia, the leaves of garlic are used in the treatment of asthma.

Bacterial Infections

Fresh garlic is said to destroy infection causing viruses and bacteria.

In addition, allicin, one of the sulphur compounds responsible for garlic's characteristic odour, is a powerful anti-bacterial and anti-viral agent that joins forces with vitamin C to help kill harmful microbes.

Raw garlic, taken orally, kills infectious bacteria in the intestines directly. Bacteria and viruses in the lungs and bronchial tract are killed by garlic's sulphur compounds, absorbed either through food, or inhalation, or poultices, and then excreted through the lungs.

Apart from lowering high blood pressure, reducing the risk of cancers of the breast, stomach and colon, serving as a diuretic, garlic also retards the growth of certain bacteria.

It also helps in the long-term treatment of intermittent claudication (restricted blood flow that causes pain while walking).

Blood Clots

Studies show that garlic is a good blood thinning agent to avoid clots that could lead to a heart attack or stroke.

Blood Disorders

A regular intake of garlic produces more natural killer cells in the blood, that will tackle infections and tumours.

Cancer

Hippocrates used garlic vapour to treat cervical cancer!

Now some case-control studies suggest that high dietary garlic consumption may be associated with decreased risks of endometrical cancers and colon cancers, as also adenomatous colorectal polyps.

Many studies have shown that as few as two or more servings of garlic per week may help protect against colon cancer.

Substances found in garlic, such as allicin, have been shown to not only protect colon cells from the toxic effects of cancer-causing chemicals, but also to stop the growth of cancer cells once they develop.

It has also been suggested that garlic may confer protection against the development of stomach cancer through its potential ability to reduce *H. pylori* induced gastritis.

Good intakes of vitamin C and selenium, with which fresh garlic is well endowed, are also associated with a reduced risk of colon cancer, making garlic a smart addition to any colon cancer prevention plan.

A recent German study disclosed that garlic compounds are toxic to malignant cells. In this study of human cells, ajoene, a garlic compound that is said to be potent, was three times as toxic to malignant cells as to normal cells.

Dr. Tin Byers of the Center for Disease Control and Prevention says that garlic might fight cancer by attacking the *H.pylori* bacteria causing the disease.

The organosulphur compound found in garlic, ajoene, may also be useful in the treatment of skin cancer.

The Archives of Dermatological Research (July 2003 issue) carries an article which states that researchers applied ajoene topically to the tumours of patients with either modular or superficial basal cell carcinoma, and in 17 of the 21 patients, the tumours shrank significantly.

The selenium in garlic not only helps prevent heart disease, but also provides protection against cancer and heavy metal toxicity.

Cardiovascular Disease

Studies have shown that garlic can suppress the growth of tumours, and is a potent antioxidant, good for cardiovascular health.

Garlic's positive cardiovascular effects are not only due to its sulphur compounds, but its vitamin C, vitamin B6, selenium and manganese.

Garlic, being a very good source of vitamin C, acts as the body's primary antioxidant defender in the bloodstream where it protects LDL cholesterol from oxidation. Since it is the oxidised form of LDL cholesterol that initiates damage to blood vessel walls, reducing levels of oxidising free radicals in the bloodstream can have a profound effect on preventing cardiovascular disease.

Cardiovascular disease is a well-known side effect of diabetes, but garlic may provide some protection, according to some latest reports. Their research results suggest that garlic may help prevent the development of abnormal vascular contraction seen in diabetes.

Cholera

The anti-bacterial action of garlic had been noticed from early days.

Its healing capacity and effectiveness against cholera have been recorded as early as 1758.

Cholesterol

In a recent study, Prof Hams Reuter, a German doctor of Cologne University, says there is a proof that garlic helps break up cholesterol in the blood vessels. Thus helping in preventing hardening of arteries that would lead to high blood pressure and heart attacks.

Other studies show that garlic can reduce LDL, or bad cholesterol.

Regular consumption of garlic decreases platelet aggregation, serum triglycerides and LDL-cholesterol levels, while increasing HDL-cholesterol and fibronolys (the process through which the body breaks up blood clots).

Studies reported in the *Annals of Internal Medicine* indicate that eating a clove of garlic a day reduces cholesterol level by 9 per cent.

Another journal, *Circulation*, sponsored by the American Heart Association, suggests that garlic may help maintain the elasticity of ageing blood vessels.

Garlic is a very good source of vitamin C, the body's primary antioxidant defender in all aqueous (water-soluble) areas, such as the bloodstream, where it protects LDL cholesterol from oxidation.

A regular intake of garlic can lower total cholesterol, while at the same time raise the good type HDL cholesterol.

Studies have shown that in adults deficient in manganese, the level of HDL cholesterol is decreased.

Cold and Cough

Laboratory studies conducted recently at the University of Munich, Germany, help explain why garlic may be such a potent remedy against common cold. In these studies it was found that garlic reduces the activity of the chemical mediator of inflammation, called nuclear transcription factor (NF) kappa-B. This mediator is itself activated as part of the immune system's inflammatory response to invading organism and damaged tissue. The sulphur fertilised garlic lowered NF kappa-B activity by a very robust 41 per cent!

In the body pain originating due to common cold and headache, taking garlic juice internally, and applying externally on the painful regions brings immediate relief.

Garlic is an excellent mucus-clearing agent. It is effective expectorant, as its allicin, which gives garlic its flavour, is converted in the body to a drug similar to Mucodyne, a classic European lung medication that regulates mucus flow.

Constipation

Garlic juice mixed with milk is an efficacious drink that relieves constipation.

Diabetes

Garlic too is known to protect against a number of the most damaging degenerative effects of diabetes, like retinopathy disease of the retina, nephropathy (kidney disease).

All these disorders are caused by an imbalance between the free radicals generated, when blood sugar levels remain high, and the body's protective antioxidant defences.

Digestive Disorders

Eating a burnt garlic is also a great remedy for indigestion.

Garlic stimulates peristaltic action and the secretion of digestive juices.

Crushed cloves of garlic may be infused in water or milk, and taken for all disorders of the digestion.

Dysentery

Garlic juice can be used to treat choleric dysentery.

Ear Disorders

Boil garlic cloves in gingelly oil for a few minutes. This oil, while still warm, should be used as ear drops in treating earache.

If there is oozing in the ears, either garlic oil or fresh juice is used as an effective ear drop.

In case there is a boil in the ear, and a throbbing pain commences, grind together garlic, radish and ginger, extract the juice, and administer a few drops in the ear. After a couple of days of application, the boil will disappear or rupture and the pain will subside.

Epilepsy

Garlic acts as a good nasal drug to rectify loss of consciousness due to epileptic fits or convulsions.

Fevers

Garlic can be used beneficially in the treatment of fevers.

Consuming garlic paste mixed with gingelly oil and salt in the morning will obviate intermittent fever, typhoid fever, and fever due to influenza.

Gastric Problems

Regular use of garlic is very effective against gastric problems.

Gout

Gout can be treated by eating *khoa* in which garlic cloves have been boiled with a little sugar.

Headaches

If you have a one-sided headache, use three drops of garlic juice, mixed with a little asafoetida powder, in the nostril on which side the head is aching.

If there is a phlegmatic collection due to this headache, relief will be experienced within five minutes.

Another method is to mix garlic juice with honey, and rub on the temple and on the side where the head is aching.

Heart Disorders

Since garlic increases HDL-cholesterol level, it helps in preventing atherosclerosis and diabetic heart disease, and reduces the risk of a heart attack or stroke.

Garlic's vitamin B6 helps prevent heart disease via another mechanism, lowering levels of homocysteine.

An intermediate product of an important cellular biochemical process called the methylation cycle, homocysteine can directly damage blood vessel walls.

In the oedemas of the heart, employing garlic is found to be very useful and mitigatory.

Garlic is said to lower blood pressure, and reduce the risk of blood clots that are responsible for most heart attacks and strokes.

Hypertension

Numerous studies also demonstrate that regular consumption of garlic lowers hypertension.

When crushed or finely chopped, it yields allicin, a powerful antibiotic and anti-fungal compound, having medical value, notably against hypertension.

Infectious Diseases

As an antiseptic, garlic is an excellent remedy for infectious diseases and inflammation of the stomach and intestine.

Influenza

Garlic juice, used as nasal drops, directly kills the viruses which causes cold or influenza.

Intestinal Disorders

Garlic acts as a worm expeller from the intestine. Fresh garlic or garlic capsules can be successfully used to treat such problems as colitis, dysentery and many other intestinal problems.

Garlic has the properties to destroy harmful bacteria in the intestines without affecting the digestion process.

Meningitis

Garlic has also been found to be effective in the treatment of meningitis, a dreaded disease affecting mostly children.

Paralysis

Garlic is effective in treating facial paralysis, paralysis of the limbs, partial paralysis, and paralysis of the thigh.

A hot tea containing garlic juice in it, and taken in the morning and evening, is useful for patients with partial paralysis.

Taken on an empty stomach, its efficacy is double-felt.

For those suffering from facial paralysis, make a *khoa* out of a litre of milk in which a few garlic cloves and a little sugar have been added, and administer it twice daily.

For paralysis of the thighs, make a paste of roasted asafoetida, cuminseed, black salt, black pepper and garlic cloves. Add a little gingelly oil, and administer it to the patient once a day.

Pneumonia

According to Dr. F. W. Crosman, if garlic is administered to pneumonia patients in sufficient quantities, they find immediate relief, bringing down the temperature, and pulse and respiration within 48 hours.

Application of garlic juice on the chest also benefits, since garlic is an irritant and, rubefacient.

Respiratory Disorders

Garlic is beneficial in curing respiratory disorders, especially whooping cough in children.

For consumption of the lungs and chronic phlegmatic collections, freshly extracted juice of garlic is useful.

Massaging of the chest with garlic oil will dissolve much of the phlegm collected within the chest.

Rheumatism

Garlic oil, massaged into aching joints, brings relief to those suffering from rheumatic pains.

A decoction of garlic taken orally is also beneficial to rheumatic and arthritic patients.

Sciatica

Garlic is equally effective in curing pains in sciatica and lumbago.

Sexual Disabilities

The inhalation of garlic oil is recommended in the case of impotency.

It is a powerful and harmless aphrodisiac food. Its regular use promotes sexual vigour and vitality.

It acts as a tonic for loss of sexual power from any cause, and for sexual debility and impotency resulting from over-indulgence in sex and nervous exhaustion from dissipating habits.

The inhalation of garlic oil or juice is recommended for sterility and impotence.

Skin Disorders

Garlic has been used successfully for a variety of skin diseases.

When you rub raw garlic over pimples several times a day, the pimples disappear, without leaving scars.

This is true even in the treatment of acne.

The process of healing is further enhanced by taking garlic orally also. This helps in purifying the bloodstream so that there is a long-term clearance of the skin.

Swallowing three garlic cloves every day helps in clearing minor skin infections quickly.

For ringworms and shingles, mix the garlic paste with pure honey, and apply on the spots. The spots will disappear without a trace, with just a few applications.

Tuberculosis

Allicin, one of the sulphur compounds responsible for garlic's characteristic odour has been shown to be effective, not only against common infections like cold, flu, stomach viruses, and candida yeast, but also against powerful pathogenic microbes including tuberculosis and botulism.

The inhalation of garlic oil is recommended in cases of tuberculosis.

Typhoid

When there is fever due to typhoid, taking garlic on an empty stomach in the morning is beneficial.

Ulcers

Frequently eating the richly-flavoured garlic may keep *H. pylori,* the bacterium responsible for most peptic ulcers, from doing much damage.

Duodenal ulcers can be cured within a few days, by taking a spoonful of garlic juice mixed with a little ghee.

Urinary Disorders

Like onions, garlic too has the diuretic property of promoting profuse urination.

The herb, leek, too is useful in setting right the disorders of urination.

Weight

The most potent and active constituent in garlic, allicin, has been shown to not only lower blood pressure, insulin and triglycerides, but also to prevent weight gain according to a study published in the *American Journal of Hypertension* (December 2003 issue).

Wounds

In vitiated wounds of the blood vessels, injecting two to three drops of pure, fresh garlic juice on the four sides of the wound gives a surprisingly useful result, as this acts as an antiseptic.

Garlic juice, with three parts of distilled water, can be employed as a lotion for cleansing infected wounds.

During World War II, garlic poultices were placed on wounds as an inexpensive, and apparently quite effective, replacement for antibiotics, which were scarce during war time.

It takes about 24-48 hours to see a substantial improvement. It also relieves pain within a short time.

Russian physicians are making extensive use of garlic in the healing of wounds.

8

Other Uses and Quick Facts

Onions

Onions are easy to grow, take up little space, and they are a staple in the kitchen. Is that enough why you should eat them, though they bring tears to your eyes?

Onions are so common place in today's society that we tend to forget their importance, and the variety of uses they have.

Uses

Onions are valuable culinary vegetables which have medicinal value.

1. *Garden Uses*

Some onion family members make ornamental contributions to the garden, including ornamental onion, chives, garlic, leek, etc.

In addition to providing a nice cottage garden look, the tops can be snipped for use in soups and salads.

Onions are important companion plants for other vegetables in the kitchen or ornamental garden.

Onions are an easy plant to grow, and require little maintenance, other than weeding, once planted.

2. *Medicinal Uses*

Onions have been used for their medicinal properties for centuries. They have anti-fungal and anti-bacterial properties, and a paste or ointment made out of them is said to prevent infection in wounds and burns.

The allicin in onions is thought to help lower blood cholesterol levels.

It also helps in stimulating the body's immune system.

Onions are thought to improve blood circulation, regulating blood pressure, preventing cardiovascular disease, and diminishing blood clots.

In sixth century India, onions were used as a diuretic. They were also considered beneficial for the heart, the eyes and the joints.

During colonial times in the United States a slice or two of wild onions was thought to be a cure for meals.

In Chinese medicine, globe onions are said to calm the liver, moisten the intestines and benefit the lungs.

Raw onions are prescribed for constipation, for lowering high blood pressure, and for healing wounds or ulcers of the skin.

Spring onions are used to induce sweating. One application for the common cold is to simmer 20 spring onions with rice to make a porridge. Add a little vinegar, and eat while it is warm. Then wrap yourself up in blankets to induce sweating.

Some health studies have shown raw onions to be effective in lowering overall cholesterol, while raising HDLs, the good cholesterol.

Additionally, onions kill infectious bacteria, help to control blood sugar, aid in dissolving blood clots, and help to prevent cancer.

At the University of California at Berkeley, researchers found that yellow and red onions, along with shallots, contain quercetin, a power antioxidant that acts as an anti-cancer agent to block the formation of cancer cells.

They also found that quercetin deactivates the growth of estrogen-sensitive cells often found to cause breast cancer .

Asthma sufferers may also benefit from a hearty dose of onions. Researchers discovered a sulphur compound contained in onions that can prevent the biochemical chain reaction which leads to asthma attacks.

Selenium, a trace mineral found in onions and garlic, has also demonstrated anti-cancer abilities.

3. *Uses in Food*

Though the onions have not yet distinguished itself in American cuisine, it certainly has in other countries. The British love their stuffed onions.

The French created onion soup, a universal favourite.

The gourmet onion tart, developed in Alsace, a north-eastern region of France.

Bhajji, a flavourful onion fritter, comes from India.

A soubise, an onion sauce or puree, also comes from the cuisine of France, and frequently accompaines lamb or mutton dishes.

Onion skins are usually considered the discards of the vegetable, but not always. Some people have discovered their powerful ability to lend a rich golden colour to soups, and to dye yarn and fabric.

The Greeks traditionally use red onion skins to dye their Easter eggs a bright pinkish red.

Fried onion rings are used to garnish French onion soup.

They are also used for decorating pulaos and biryanis.

The Gibson, an alcoholic drink like a martini, requires a small pickled onion.

4. *Nutritional Benefits*

If you are counting calories, you might want to take advantage of the low-calorie content of sweet raw onions. With half a cup of chopped raw onions, you will tally up a mere 30 calories. If you cook these same onions, you are up to only 46 calories.

Be sure to include spring onions in your salads frequently for their high calcium, potassium and magnesium scores.

And don't forget the powerful antioxidants delivered by onion. Quercetin has anti-cancer agents.

Garlic

A note to garlic lovers looking for all excuses to eat more: You may have to eat a lot of raw garlic to experience its benefits, as many as 5-10 cloves a day—a prospect that may drive your friends away! Luckily, many garlic supplements offer an odour-free alternative.

Uses

Uses in Food

Garlic, onions and leeks are very versatile. Eat them raw, braised, boiled, steamed, baked, sautéed, scalloped, fried or grilled.

They can serve as a vegetable or a seasoning.

Whichever way you choose, uncover the treasures of good health and good flavour found in these ancient foods by including onions, garlic and leeks in your menus.

It will pay us handsomely to consider this pod because it is one of the nature's great masterpieces as a safe and certain remedy for many of man's serious and devastating diseases.

This wonderful herb has been used from very ancient times, both as food and medicine.

Medicinal Uses

Garlic is a plant with a long history of use not only as a food, but also as a folk medicine.

The list of past medicinal uses of garlic is very long, but most interesting are the claims that eating garlic reduces heart problems.

Garlic is one of the oldest medicinal remedies known to man which has been cultivated and used from time immemorial in the treatment of many diseases.

Both its romantic history and its very remarkable reactive virtues are vastly interesting and educational to all earnest and honest physicians.

It is notable that it stands out today as one of our greatest and most important therapeutic agents.

It is alterative, diaphoretic, diuretic, expectorant, antispasmodic, antihistamic, stimulant, antiseptic, disinfectant, tonic, nervine, antiphthisic, germicide and vermicide.

Medically speaking, the most important compound in garlic is allicin, which is changed via several pathways into ajoene and thioacrolein.

Scientists have substantiated that especially ajoene is a strong antithrombotic factor, that is, it increases the length of time it takes for blood to clot. This is important in preventing heart disease, in which blood clots become lodged in blood vessels, causing strokes.

Oils extracted from garlic definitely interfere with agglutination of blood platelets.

In garlic, the allicin also acts as an antifungal agent, thereby stopping fungi from attacking the fleshy bulb.

Being part of the onion family, garlic is one of the longest-standing natural medicines. Liberal uses of it may contribute to the lower incidence of heart disease of people with a Mediterranean diet.

The allicin in garlic has natural antibiotic and antifungal properties.

Allicin is believed to help maintain a healthy heart by stimulating the immune system and lowering the blood cholestrol as well as reducing blood clotting.

Garlic juice works as an antibiotic on wounds.

Garlic may not do much for your breath, but perhaps no other herb can do more for the health of your heart than garlic.

German health authorities have approved garlic as a primary defence against atherosclerosis (the build-up of fatty plaques on artery walls that can lead to heart disease) and high cholesterol levels. A 1999 German study showed an 18 per cent reduction in plaque build-up in the arteries of people who took 900 mg of garlic powder every day. There was also a 13 per cent reduction in triglycerides, another type of fat found in the blood.

The sulphides in garlic decreases the tendency for blood clots to form, plus they lower the levels of LDL cholesterol, and decrease total cholesterol.

A dose of garlic in the diet may help to prevent hardening of the aorta, the major artery that carries blood from the heart.

The active substances, allyl sulphides, provide protection against cancer.

Garlic is also used as an effective treatment against bacteria, fungi and viruses.

In Russia, garlic is being tested as a treatment for arthritis.

Ingesting aged garlic extract may provide nutritional support for the health of those suffering from a wide range of vascular conditions, including ischemia, inflammatory diseases, diabetes and athersclerosis.

The aged garlic extract significantly boosts the body's natural disease fighters—antioxidants.

Also be aware that this potent herb is a natural blood thinner.

It is effective in arresting intestinal putrefaction.

It is beneficially used against contagious diseases, hypertension, fevers, parasites, worms, colic and nicotine poisoning.

In old days, garlic was employed as a specific for leprosy, psoriasis and several forms of skin diseases.

It was also believed to have most beneficial results in smallpox, applied to the soles of the feet.

It has been authoritatively reported that tuberculosis has been successfully treated by inhalation of the freshly extracted juice of garlic, diluted with equal quantities of water.

Another instance of the remarkable penetrating power of garlic is the fact that the juice of fresh garlic mixed with olive oil, and rubbed on the chest, throat and between the shoulder blades gives great relief in whooping cough, asthma, dyspnoea and bronchitis.

Quick Facts and Tips

Onion

1. Adding an onion to most savoury food can boost the health benefits as well as add flavour.
2. Onions can be eaten raw or cooked, but they taste sweeter when cooked, especially if cooked slowly.
3. Gently fry onions with some herbs, and add fresh vegetable stock to make a tasty soup.
4. Do not use a food processor when chopping green onions. The onions will become mushy.
5. Create a garnish by slicing the tops of green onions in half lengthwise, without slicing the bulb. Place the onion in a bowl of ice water. After a few hours the onion green will begin to curl. Remove from cold water, and use as a garnish for a salad.

6. Add onion flavour to a dish without including onion pieces, by squeezing a half onion on a lemon squeezer.

7. Light one or two candles in the area you are cutting the onions to prevent tears.

8. To remove the onion odour from your hand rub a piece of lemon in salt, and then squeeze the juice on your hands, rub the juice in, and then rinse it off.

9. How delightful is the addition of half-moon slices of sweet onions to a salad of crisp mixed greens.!

Garlic

1. Use crushed garlic as a general seasoning when cooking to reduce salt intake and add flavour.

2. Add finely-crushed garlic to salad dressings dips or salsa.

3. Use in stir-fries with peppers, oily fish and olive oil.